TO MY DAD, JACK, WHO CAN MAKE ANYONE LAUGH. —CM

Dogplay

The Canine Guide to Being Happy

Photographs by KIM LEVIN

Written by CHRISTINE MONTAQUILA

STEWART, TABORI & CHANG • NEW YORK

Published in 2010 by Stewart, Tabori & Chang
An imprint of ABRAMS

ISBN: 978-1-58479-827-9

Editor: Dervla Kelly
Designer: Susi Oberhelman
Production Manager: Tina Cameron

The text of this book was composed in Gotham Rounded and Postino.

Printed and bound in China

10 9 8 7 6 5 4 3 2 1

ABRAMS
THE ART OF BOOKS SINCE 1949
115 West 18th Street
New York, NY 10011
www.abramsbooks.com

Remember **life** isn't a **busy contest**.

MONTE

Watch more **reality** and less reality **TV**.

BUSTER

Stop counting **years** and **dress sizes.**

MICA

If you want it, **get off** your butt and go **get it**.

On your list of **must-haves**, put loyalty up there with **ice cream**.

BART

Reinvent yourself every decade or so.

AUDREY & WATSON

Explore new **backyards**,

but know your **way home**.

BAYONNE

Don't **microanalyze** every nice breeze

that comes **your way**.

MAX

air

God's **prozac**.

OLIVER

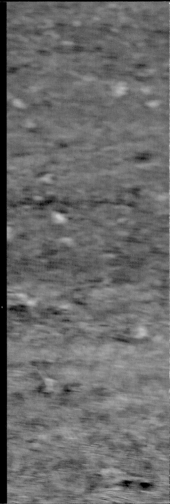

When you want to **change** your attitude,

change your **time zone**.

REILLY & NOAH

Be **grateful** for the **life** right

under **your nose**.

coco

Become a pathological **optimist**.

OZZEY

Don't **be afraid** to occasionally

be the **punch line**.

MARCELLA & TARA

Protect, defend, and **frolic**

with a **vengeance.**

BLUE

Develop a **love/love** relationship with **food**.

 TONKA

Never **miss** an **appointment** with **a couch**.

SMACKERS

Treat **love** like a big **perfume** ad.

BRANDY & JAKE

Be more **reliable** than the **postal service**.

LUCY

Relive the best parts of your **childhood**.

VIOLET

Give inner **peace** a **chance**.

MAGOO

Enjoy more **solitary**

and less **confinement**.

RILEY

Master the art of the **boondoggle**.

LULU

If life insists on handing you **drama**,

be the **star**.

NOAH

Know when to be a **don't-do-it-yourselfer.**

SCARLETT

Tap into the **mind/body/snack** connection.

ROSIE

Firmly believe that **neurotic**

equals **charming**.

OPAL

Be a **lover** and a **fighter**,

just not at the **same time**.

TILLY

Consider yourself a **vacationista**.

 TUCK

Acknowledgments

Many thanks to Dervla Kelly and her new addition. To Rick for putting up with us and being our legal guru. And to the many kind and patient dog owners who allowed their dogs to be a part of this project. We know you get it.

About the Authors

By day, **CHRISTINE MONTAQUILA** is a freelance writer and co-creator of Naughty Betty, a greeting card and gift company. She lives outside Chicago with her husband, three children, Luca, Francesca, and Leo, and their gray tiger cat, Maddie. Visit her at www.naughtybettyinc.com.

KIM LEVIN has published 18 books including the bestselling *Cattitude* and *Why We Love Dogs*. Her other pet portrait books include *Frenemies*, *PhoDOGraphy*, *Pawfiles*, *Caternal Instincts*, *Catrimony*, *Hounds for the Holidays*, *Why We Love Cats*, *Growing Up*, *Dogma*, and *Working Dogs*. Her company Bark & Smile Pet Portraits combines her passion for photography and her love of animals. An advocate of animal adoption, Kim has been donating her photography services for many years. Kim lives in New Jersey with her husband, two children, Ian and Rachael, and their dog, Charlie. You can view her work at www.kimlevin.com.

For more work by Kim and Christine, including their line of pet-themed greeting cards called Molly & Fig, visit www.mollyandfig.com.